The Light of Love

Henry's Journey

FanatiXx Publication
D9, Seth Deokarandas Complex, Kachery Road, Rourkela
ISO 9001:2015 CERTIFIED
Website: www.fanatixxpublication.com

© **Copyright, 2022,** Karan Manchanda

All rights reserved. No part of this book may be reproduced, stored in a retrieval system, or transmitted, in any form by any means, electronic, mechanical, magnetic, optical, chemical, manual, photocopying, recording or otherwise, without prior written consent of the author.

The Light of Love : Henry's Journey
By: Karan Manchanda
ISBN: 978-93-5605-911-5
1st Edition

Price: 199.00 INR
Printed and Typeset by: BooksClub.in

The opinions/ contents expressed in this book are solely of the author and do not represent the opinions/ stands/ thoughts of FanatiXx.

DISCLAIMER

All rights reserved. This book may not be reproduced in whole or in part, or transmitted in any form, without written permission from the publisher, nor may any part of this book be reproduced, stored in a retrieval system, or transmitted in any form or by any means electronic, mechanical, photocopying, microfilming, and recording without written permission from the publisher.

Author assures that all content is original and he/she has full rights to publish and distribute the same. In any case of plagiarism, the publisher is not liable.

About the Author:

Karan Manchanda, a renowned astrologer and life coach, hails from the vibrant city of New Delhi, India. At 34 years of age, Karan has established himself as a trusted guide and mentor to thousands of individuals worldwide, steering them through life's challenges with his profound insights and accurate predictions.

With a strong foundation in education and experience, Karan's journey into the realms of astrology and life coaching was a path paved with dedication and purpose. Initially embarking on a career as a tutor, Karan's thirst for knowledge led him to pursue an MBA in finance, where he honed his skills in the intricate workings of the stock market. His corporate experience further enriched his understanding of the complexities of the business world before he followed his intuition and embraced a career in astrology.

Karan firmly believes in the fusion of theoretical knowledge and practical application, a philosophy that has shaped his approach to helping others find clarity and direction in their lives. His groundbreaking predictions, such as foreseeing significant events like Donald Trump's victory in 2016 and the Brexit outcome, have cemented his reputation as a visionary in the field of astrology.

Beyond his professional accomplishments, Karan is a man of strong family values, finding solace and strength in the bonds of kinship. He advocates for personal growth and resilience through his unique concept called "Befour," which underscores the importance of grounding oneself in the fundamental elements of facts, observation, understanding, and resilience.

Karan's mission is to empower individuals to navigate life's uncertainties with grace, adaptability, and a steadfast commitment to self-discovery. Through his work, he continues to inspire others to embrace life's challenges as opportunities for growth, guiding them towards a brighter and more fulfilling future.

https://linktr.ee/Astro_Karan

Contents

Chapter 1: 7

A Haunting Past At 68 7

Chapter 2: 11

The Lonely Road 11

Chapter 3: 15

Meeting Lisa At 31 15

Chapter 4: 19

Blossoming Love 19

Chapter 5: 23

A New Purpose 23

Chapter 6: 27

The Unthinkable Loss 27

Chapter 7: 31

Reflection and Legacy 31

Chapter 8: 35

The Eternal Connection 35

Chapter 1:

A Haunting Past At 68

Henry, now a world-famous scientist, reflects on his childhood trauma. His parents died when he was just three years old, and his uncle and aunt took him in. They were kind to him until the birth of their daughter when he was 11. After that, the love and care vanished. At age 12, Henry faced abuse from a friend of his uncle, causing immense trauma. The school was no better, as he was bullied relentlessly.

Lesson: The foundation for resilience is being laid in the darkest times. The past may shape us, but it does not define our future.

Chapter 2:

The Lonely Road

Despite personal struggles, Henry excelled academically. His escape was through books and learning, which eventually led him to a career in science. His personal life, however, remained barren. He felt like a victim, forever scarred by his past.

Lesson: Intellectual achievement is valuable, but emotional healing requires more than knowledge and passion.

Chapter 3:

Meeting Lisa At 31

Henry moved into a new neighborhood and met Lisa, his neighbor who was seven years younger. Lisa remembered him from school as the shy boy who kept to himself. She was kind, compassionate, and full of life. She saw beyond his scars and reached out to him.

Lesson: Genuine connections can heal deep wounds and foster self-belief, and sometimes, it takes someone else's belief in us to start believing in ourselves.

Chapter 4:
Blossoming Love

Lisa and Henry began spending more time together. She brought hope and love into his life, teaching him to see the beauty in the world and himself. They fell deeply in love and eventually married. Lisa's unwavering support and belief in him transformed Henry's outlook on life

Lesson: Love has the power to heal and transform, providing a safe space to confront and overcome inner demons.

Chapter 5:

A New Purpose

With Lisa by his side, Henry's work flourished. He made groundbreaking discoveries and innovations, driven by a desire to escape his past and a newfound purpose and passion for life. Lisa's belief that problems exist within us and how we overcome them is important became his guiding principle.

Lesson: Love and support fuel our purpose and passion, propelling us to greatness.

Chapter 6:

The Unthinkable Loss

Tragedy struck when Lisa passed away at the age of 48. Henry was devastated but found solace in their shared love and memories. He kept her spirit alive in his heart, talking to her every day.

Lesson: Love transcends physical existence and can guide and inspire even after a loved one is gone.

Chapter 7:

Reflection and Legacy

Henry gave a heartfelt speech reflecting on his journey on the day of his retirement. He emphasized the importance of love and care and how they can change a person's life, speaking of his transformative past and Lisa's profound impact on him.

Lesson: Our past does not define us; how we choose to overcome it shapes our future.

Chapter 8:

The Eternal Connection

Even in retirement, Henry continued to innovate and inspire, dedicating his work to Lisa's memory. He found peace knowing she was always with him, guiding him with her love. Her love had given him the strength to overcome his past and achieve greatness.

Lesson: True love never dies and stays with us, guiding and inspiring us throughout our lives. Epilogue: A Life Transformed Henry's story is one of transformation and resilience, teaching us that no matter how dark our past is, the light of love and hope can lead us to a brighter future.

Final Lesson: Life is a journey of transformation. With love, hope, and resilience, we can overcome any obstacle and find the meaning and purpose we seek.

www.ingramcontent.com/pod-product-compliance
Lightning Source LLC
LaVergne TN
LVHW061605070526
838199LV00077B/7178